BlockChain

How Bitcoin and Blockchain are changing the economic world. Blockchain, what problem does it solve?

Table of Contents

Introduction

Chapter One: What is Blockchain?

Chapter Two: Blockchain's Future

Chapter Three: The Difference Between Blockchain and Bitcoin

Chapter Four: What Is Bitcoin?

Chapter Five: Who Controls Bitcoin?

Chapter Six: How Coins Are Created

Chapter Seven: Mining Bitcoin

Chapter Eight: Buying and Selling Bitcoin

Chapter Nine: Wallets

Chapter Ten: Pros and Cons of Blockchain

Chapter Eleven: Blockchain and the Financial Industry

Chapter Twelve: Blockchain Hard Forks

Chapter Thirteen: Blockchain and Other Industries

Chapter Fourteen: The Impact of Blockchain

Conclusion

Description

© Copyright 2018 by Dan Wilson - All rights reserved.

The following eBook is reproduced below with the goal of providing information that is as accurate and reliable as possible. The following eBook is reproduced with the goal of providing information that is accurate and reliable as possible. Nevertheless, both the publisher and the writer are not experts on the topic that would be discussed. It is highly recommended that further research be done. Professionals should be consulted, if necessary before undertaking any of the action endorsed herein.

This declaration is deemed fair and valid by both the American Bar Association and the Committee of Publishers Association and is legally bonded throughout the United States.

Furthermore, the transmission, duplication, or reproduction of any of the following work including specific information will be considered an illegal act irrespective of the mode the act was done. This extends to the creation of secondary, tertiary or a recorded copy. Such acts are only allowed with a written consent from the publisher on hand. All additional rights reserved.

The information in the following pages is considered to be an accurate account of facts, and as such any inattention, use or misuse of the information by the reader, makes them solely responsible for their action. In case the reader experienced damages upon following what is discussed here, the publisher or the original author of this work is free of liability.

Additionally, the information in the following pages is intended only to impart knowledge, and should thus be thought of as universal. As befitting its nature, it is presented without assurance regarding its continued validity or interim quality. Trademarks that are mentioned are done without written consent and should not be considered an endorsement from the trademark holder.

Introduction

Congratulations on downloading *Blockchain: Everything You Need to Know About Blockchain*, and thank you for doing so!

The following chapters will discuss every aspect of blockchain that you need to know so that you can use blockchain efficiently.

Blockchain is the platform cryptocurrency operates. Think of blockchain as the foundation of cryptocurrency. Having a solid foundation regarding blockchain is vital so that you wouldn't have to worry about building something and see it all fall apart because you lack knowledge on the subject.

There are various blockchain applications that you will read about in this book. However, if you want to learn more about these applications, you can find them online. Do not assume that you know everything by reading one book. While you will get the information you need in this book, you should never stop learning about the platforms and applications you are using.

There are plenty of books on this subject on the market, thanks again for choosing this one! Every effort was made to ensure it is full of as much useful information as possible. Please enjoy!

Chapter One: What is Blockchain?

"The blockchain is an incorruptible digital ledger of economic transactions that can be programmed to record not just financial transactions, but virtually anything of value." – Don and Alex Tapscott

When you are thinking about blockchain, you should think about it as an Excel spreadsheet duplicated tens of thousands of times, so that it is spread across an extensive network of computers. Now, imagine that the system was created so that it would update the spreadsheet on a regular basis. After you have pictured that, you will have an accurate and basic understanding of blockchain.

Any information that is placed on a blockchain will exist as a database that is continuously reconciled and shared by thousands if not millions of computers throughout the world. Using the network will have its benefits, such as the blockchain database not being stored in a specific location so that it is public and easy to verify. A central authority does not exist, thus the system is harder to hack. Blockchain, along with its data will be accessible to anyone who has access to the internet.

Whenever a transaction is completed on the blockchain, it undergoes verification for it to be accepted on a block in the chain. Each block will work off of the previous block. And each transaction has its own block which makes it easier for a user to locate a transaction once it has been accepted by the system.

How does blockchain work?

As stated earlier, blockchain will work based on a shared public ledger that the entire network relies on. Every transaction that is confirmed will be included on the blockchain. With this, wallets will be able to calculate their spendable balance along with how much is owed to the user that verified the transaction.

To keep blockchain safe, cryptography is heavily enforced. Cryptography is a set of mathematical equations which allow users to create proofs while providing a high level of security. The great thing about cryptography is that it gives the user the assurance that their wallet cannot be hacked since it is password protected.

Any transaction that occurs between two wallets will also be included on the blockchain. Blockchain wallets will have a private key which works as a proof that you're the one who performed the transaction.

Signatures can also perform the private key's function. All transactions will be broadcasted among users and will typically take ten minutes to be confirmed.

Chapter Two: Blockchain's Future

There has been a lot of interest in blockchain since it came out, and that interest has increased as the year progresses—a proof that blockchain is changing the world of technology as we know it.

However, no one is sure of the blockchain's future. There are predictions regarding its future; however, only time can tell as blockchain evolves.

For now, let's look at a few predictions regarding blockchain's future.

1. The financial industry will adapt blockchain first.

Since the roots of blockchain are in cryptocurrency, any financial firm is most likely going to be the first to use the new technology. PwC's 2017 Global Digital IQ Survey discovered that around nine percent of the businesses offering financial services were already making investments in blockchain, and thirty-six percent of the businesses are planning to invest in the next three years.

2. More blockchain uses are on the way.

While financial firms will be the first to experiment with blockchain; they are not going to be the only ones. Other industries already took the risk of experimenting with blockchain. The industries comprising the 11% which utilizes blockchain before the financial firms include hospitality or leisure companies, automotive (6%), healthcare (12%), energy and mining (7%), other retailers (6%), and technology (7%). These industries would be joined by more in the upcoming years.

3. Various countries are trying to figure out how to regulate blockchain.

Most governments have no established rules in order to govern blockchain applications or any other type of cryptocurrency, and this is both a blessing and a curse for those blockchain advocates. When you look at it from one side, you will see that startups will be free to innovate however they wish. But, on the other hand, some of the more established companies will be hesitant to use the technology due to the fact that there are no regulations and there is too much risk when they do decide to invest on blockchain.

Various governments and international organizations are working on regulating blockchain. An example of this is Japan upon realizing that Bitcoin is a legal currency. A study published by the WEF looked on how Bitcoin would be affected when blockchain is under regulations.

In the United States, there are some agencies, such as the IRS and the Federal Election Commission that has policies covering every aspect of cryptocurrency and blockchain. It appears that the United States and other countries will continue to find a way to regulate blockchain, and once they do, they will pass the legislation to make it permanent.

4. Investors will continue to fund startups on blockchain.

Capitalists who wanted to fund startups on blockchain increase. Coindesk found that investors have put almost 1.8 billion dollars in the market. During 2016, blockchain startups were able to obtain 501 million dollars fund while this year about 303 million dollars was added.

Not every startup will work on blockchain. At the same time, there are established firms that have blockchain projects as well. So, there is a little bit of everything for everyone on blockchain.

5. Ethereum will grow in importance.

One of the most significant blockchain projects you have most likely heard about is Ethereum. Ethereum tends to confuse someone because it is not only a cryptocurrency but also a platform that is used when creating blockchain-based applications, like smart contracts. CoinDesk's report on the state of blockchain found out that 94% of blockchain enthusiasts have positive feedback about Ethereum. The said report also pointed out that the market cap on Ethereum increased to 499% from the last quarter of 2016 to the first quarter of 2017.

6. Standard organizations and companies will push for blockchain interoperability.

One of the biggest things that the Enterprise Ethereum Alliance, The Wall Street Blockchain Alliance, and Hyperledger are focusing on is the development of standards that will make blockchain interoperable. When companies have the ability to coalesce around a specific rule, then the rate of accepting blockchain-based payments, solutions, and currency would increase.

CoinDesk's statement regarding blockchain is as follows, "As more and more blockchains, cryptocurrencies, tokens, and distributed ledger systems launch and prosper, it's becoming [increasingly] obvious that we have created a whole new web of decentralized technologies, forming the backbone of an entirely new economy, information network, and source of truth. We have seen a push and trend towards interoperability to take full advantage of the several innovations across the ecosystem."

7. New technology will make blockchain faster and more scalable.

There are a lot of technological companies that are trying to find more ways to make blockchain transactions faster and more scalable. The two most notable efforts in finding a solution to this problem include Raiden and Lightning.

8. The demand for blockchain talent will increase.

The demand for developers and others who know blockchain will increase as the technology takes off. But, only a few universities offer blockchain courses, so as the technology and demand increases, this may increase as well.

9. Blockchain is becoming more critical to markets that are emerging.

The last prediction for the future of blockchain deals with the impact that it will have on emerging markets. Vinay Gupta and Rob Knight (writers for the Harvard Business Review) have theorized that blockchain and cryptocurrency will help these markets by leapfrogging past the economies that are more developed.

In Africa, when cell technology became more common over the landline services; a suggestion was made that in a way blockchain would make banking in areas possible for those that cannot be reached by traditional financial services.

It is not clear if the theories will come to fruition or not, but it is likely that blockchain will have a major impact on the global economy.

Chapter Three: The Difference Between Blockchain and Bitcoin

It isn't often that you hear blockchain and bitcoin apart. But, they are two separate entities, and you need to know the difference between the two in order to understand how to use both. In this chapter, you will learn those differences.

Upon observing a bitcoin network in operation, a lot of users decide that they will be able to use this technology to secure other data types. Bitcoin is built on a blockchain-based network that will secure other cryptocurrencies and data that has nothing to do with bitcoin at all. Some examples of blockchain-based systems are decentralized app platforms, smart contracts, and many more.

So, the word bitcoin refers to a currency token that exists only on the bitcoin network.

Blockchain technology is any project utilized for the verification of a chain of data blocks.

Therefore, blockchain will be the system where these projects will take place. One of those projects will be bitcoin which uses bitcoin currency.

In the end, blockchain will be a database that holds all of the transactions. Bitcoin is not going to have any transactions in its system because they are all going to be placed inside of the blockchain.

The important thing to remember is that blockchain is the foundation and everything else is built on top of it.

Chapter Four: What Is Bitcoin?

Bitcoin is a digital currency created in 2009 by the Satoshi Nakamoto group. A transaction will be completed without the need of a middleman. No transaction fees and real names will be needed for the system to work! Therefore, it is completely safe for you to use. More merchants are trying to accept Bitcoin, thus you will be able to use your cryptocurrency stash to buy your family pizza or spoil yourself and get a manicure!

You will want to consider using Bitcoin because you can make purchases and remain completely anonymous. On top of that, making international payments are cheaper and easier, since regulations are nonexistent. Most small businesses will want to use Bitcoin because a fee is not required when accepting credit cards.

How Bitcoin works?

Bitcoin uses blockchain – a public ledger that the entire Bitcoin network will rely on. A Bitcoin transaction involves a transfer of Bitcoin tokens between two Bitcoin wallets that are on the blockchain. These wallets contain a secret piece of data known as a private key.

You will use the private key to sign the transaction, thereby providing a mathematical proof that you are indeed the user and owner of the wallet. The said signature will also assist in preventing a transaction from being altered after it has been issued to a user. Each transaction will be broadcasted between the users on the blockchain, while the network confirms the transaction and places it on the blockchain.

Why was Bitcoin created?

Bitcoin was developed in order to perform transactions not governed and regulated by the government or any other central authority. By creating Bitcoin, Satoshi Nakamoto was able to make cryptocurrency which in turn lowered purchasing costs for users and businesses. On top of that, cryptocurrency is digital which makes it accessible. Once Bitcoin is purchased or sent, then it is placed in the new account instantly.

Chapter Five: Who Controls Bitcoin?

If Bitcoin is not controlled by a central authority, then who manages it?

The answer is easy-- every Bitcoin user around the world controls Bitcoin!

The Bitcoin developers are continually working in improving the software, but they are not successful in enforcing the rules of Bitcoin since all users get to choose the software they use. In order to remain compatible with each version of the software utilized by Bitcoin users, Bitcoin is limited in working with a complete consensus that occurs among all users. This gives all users and developers a strong incentive to adapt to the new protocols and protect the consensus.

Bitcoin users have the power to choose what they want to do with their coins, and no one else will be able to tell them what to do. Also, no one will be able to take your coins away from you unless your wallet is hacked, thus making it possible to steal your coins. This may also occur if the exchange is hacked and this is where you keep your coins. Therefore, it is not recommended that you leave your coins in the exchange because it can be hacked. With this, your wallet needs to have a strong password to keep it secure.

The reason that Bitcoins are controlled by their users goes back to why Bitcoins were created in the first place. The group who first created Bitcoins did not want to create a currency that could be controlled by the government. However, this does not stop the government from attempting to find a way to manage it, anyway.

Chapter Six: How Coins Are Created

One block on the blockchain will be rewarded with about fifty Bitcoins per block, and it will remain that way until 210,000 blocks have been mined. Once the system reaches 210,001, the reward will be cut down to twenty-five coins a block.

Changing the difficulty of Bitcoin is impossible since it is set up to ensure that a block is found every ten minutes. This means that if ten minutes is spent on blocks being created, then a block being halved will happen every four years. So, following that logic means that new Bitcoins are created every ten minutes. Therefore, anyone will be able to verify when a new Bitcoin is created.

Sooner or later, the rewards for blocks will half themselves so much that the rewards become so small to the point that no new coins are created.

The only Bitcoins that can be spent are the ones are rewarded to miners which make it impossible for a user to bring new Bitcoins into the supply. And, this is due to cryptography whose function is verifying all the transactions occurring on the Bitcoin blockchain.

A Bitcoin user is required to input the correct digital signature so that they can spend their Bitcoins. A miner will need to verify the process by providing their proof of work. Proof of work prevents someone from spending Bitcoin value tokens which they do not own, Moreover, proof of work also prevents users from creating a Bitcoin that is not issued through the Bitcoin network.

It is possible for a user to create their own fork of Bitcoin whose function is to produce new coins. However, the newly created will only be valid on the new fork since the main Bitcoin blockchain will see these new coins as invalid.

The value of Bitcoin

In December of 2017, Bitcoin hit a new high of $19,990!

With the new all-time high, the investors who purchased their Bitcoins a year ago rejoiced because they made a profit. In 2016, the price of Bitcoin became $572 per token, which was less than half the price of an ounce of gold. Therefore, if an investor decided that they were going to invest $100, they would have a profit of $3400 that year.

But, it is vital to remember that Bitcoins are highly volatile and can easily lose or gain up to $200 in a day. Analysts from Goldman Sachs are preparing for the price of cryptocurrency to fall in the nearby future before it starts to go up once again.

Because of the sudden rise of Bitcoin, it is compared with other investments which shot up only to fall well below their average in the previous years, such as tech stocks (in the late 1990s), or even the real estate in the early years of the 2000s.

Much like watching the tremendous gains that you can get from a Power Ball jackpot, Main Street investors were advised to not get wrapped up in Bitcoin investments. "It's really, really not worth it for the ordinary consumer," a professor at Troy University told MONEY early in 2017.

On the other hand, Bitcoin advocates say that Bitcoin will continue to go up. Founder of the Bitcoin Foundation, Charlie Shrem, has been reported saying that he thinks Bitcoins are cheap when every Bitcoin costs $100,000.

So, it is hard to say what the value of Bitcoin will be in the future because the prices rise and fall with the market. But keep in mind that what goes up must always come down. This means that while the market is up, you may want to sell your Bitcoins so that you can hang onto your profit. But, if you do not want to, you can hold on to them and spend them elsewhere. Do not be surprised though when you lose money because you decided to hold onto them.

Chapter Seven: Mining Bitcoin

Mining is not an easy process because most people have coding experience by now. But, there are still those who don't have experience in coding and systems, such as Linux or Ubuntu. Therefore, they need a beginner's guide in mining. And, that is what you will find in this chapter!

1. Obtain a Bitcoin mining rig.

Mining Bitcoins is a competitive niche to try and break into since most miners are equipped with the latest mining hardware. Before you start mining, you need to do your due diligence. In other words, you need to do the math and figure out if mining will be profitable for you in the long run.

The best way to do this is to use a Bitcoin mining calculator. All you will do is enter the data of the miner that you are planning to purchase and see if it is possible for you to break even or make a profit. But, from experience, if you do not get at least $200 extra dollars, then it is not going to be worth it because you are not going to be getting any Bitcoins.

After you have completed your calculations, you will need to get your miner. You should make sure to look at the mining hardware reviews so that you can get the best miner for you. As of October 13, 2017, the most powerful miner is Antminer S9.

Note: it is possible to mine with your graphics card, but because of how competitive mining has gotten, having an ASIC miner will give you a better chance to compete and get Bitcoins.

2. Find a Bitcoin wallet.

You will need to find a Bitcoin wallet because Bitcoin is an internet-based currency and you need to have a location to store your currency. Once you have gotten your wallet, you need to get your wallet address. This address will be a long series of letters and numbers. Each wallet will contain a different public address that will be put into the box to have Bitcoins sent to them. The private key will be the key that gives you access to your wallet so that you are the only one who can get the coins sitting in your wallet.

If you decide to use a self-hosted wallet, there is an extra step that you will need to go through. This step involves copying your wallet data onto a thumb drive and then placing that thumb drive in a safe location. By doing this, you will have a copy of your wallet in case your computer crashes.

3. Locate a mining pool.

Now that you have your wallet, you will need to join a mining pool. Mining pools are composed of a group of miners that use their combined computing power to make more Bitcoins. If you to choose to mine alone, you will be getting rewards but fewer and rarer than when you are in a group.

In a pool, you will be given small algorithms to solve, and each person who completes his algorithm will earn coins. So, if you are consistent about your worth, then you will receive a decent amount of Bitcoins, and then mining is definitely going to be worth your while.

Before joining a pool, ask yourself these questions:

1. How is the reward system set up?

2. How stable is the pool that you are looking at?

3. Are there any fees for mining or pulling out funds?

4. What are the stats for the pool as a whole?

5. How frequently does the pool find a block? (How often a block is located determines how often you will be rewarded.)

6. Is it easy to pull your funds out?

4. Download a mining program

After you have gotten the basics down, you will be ready to mine. But first, find a mining client that can run on your computer for you to have control on your mining rig. The software that you need depends on the rig that you bought. Most mining pools have their own software, such as Bitminer, but there are some pools that do not have any software which meant that you can use any software you want.

5. Start mining

At this point in time, hopefully, you have everything and ready to start. Make sure you connect your miner to a power supply and turn it on. You should also make sure you link it through a USB connection to your computer before you open your mining software. The first step is to join your pool by placing your username and password into the appropriate fields.

Allow your computer to configure before you start mining for Bitcoins. You will have the option of starting a collection share to represent your work when it comes to finding the next block to be worked on. Depending on the rules of the pool, you will be paid for all of the work that you do, but the only way to get your coins is to put your address upon joining your pool.

There are a lot of people that are still unsure about how fiat currency is centralized, while digital currencies are decentralized. If you do not clearly understand the differences, then you are not going to be able to see the benefits of both options.

One comment that you have most likely heard about fiat currency is that it is printed on demand. There are a lot of people that believe this statement is overrated because every governing body will have the option of creating fiat currency "out of thin air." But, this goes without saying that if you increase the supply of fiat that is backed by a previous value, then all the money that is currently in circulation will lose value.

Fiat currency is back up by an asset to create an illusion of value. The truth is that the US Dollar does not have a back up by an actual asset in a long time. The truth is, the US currency in circulation is founded on the faith of the people in their government, but really, it does not have any intrinsic value.

Furthermore, any new money placed in circulation is not going to have any value. But still, new money is being printed, and then distributed to one of the twelve Federal Reserve Banks. There are two

Federal Reserve Banks that are privately owned, this just means that there is no transparency in an ecosystem where only a handful of people determine the wealth of the entire nation.

Upon realizing that the Federal Reserve Bank is privately owned, then you will also realize that financial institutions will do whatever they want because there is no government overseer. And, because of these privately-owned banks, there have been several economic crises that have happened over the years.

The last thing you need to know about the Federal Reserve is that they can create new money whenever they feel like, as long as they purchase a Treasury bond. The other option that they have is to use a loan that they bought with the purpose of financing all of the debt in the United States.

Bitcoin has a supply of about 21 million coins making it the most popular digital currency in the world. Since no other coins will be allowed to be placed in circulation, the coins that are in circulation have some kind of value, and there is the possibility that the value will increase over time. Bitcoin investors believe that all of the Bitcoins will be mined by the year 2140.

Speaking of creating new Bitcoins, there is no institute that can print additional funds. The only way that extra coins can be placed in circulation is through the mining process. Miners will be given rewards for bringing new coins into circulation, and they are also going to be given the privilege of spending these coins first.

Until the last Bitcoin is mined, anyone can participate in the mining of Bitcoins. There is not a process that you will need to go through to mine since Bitcoin works off of an open ecosystem. But, all funds will be controlled by the people that are active in the ecosystem, and this alone this helps in creating a decentralized system.

On top of that, Bitcoin does not have a point of failure which makes the network completely tamper-proof. Unlike fiat currency, a central authority responsible for controlling the supply of Bitcoin is nonexistent, thus making Bitcoin consumer- driven. Additionally, Bitcoin has several points of distribution when it comes to the mining process.

The last thing to keep in mind is that when Bitcoins are spent, they will be placed back into the Bitcoin's economy. By spending fiat currency, it will be kept out of the economy until a bank gets a hold of it again, and that can take several years.

The most significant difference between fiat currency and digital currencies, like Bitcoin, is that they are self-sustainable which is better for everyone involved!

Chapter Eight: Buying and Selling Bitcoin

To get Bitcoin, you have the option of buying and selling the value token. When you purchase Bitcoin, you are obviously inserting the value token into your Bitcoin wallet, so that you can spend it at a later date. But, if you will sell Bitcoin, you can obtain fiat currency or other cryptocurrencies.

In this section, you will learn the process of buying and selling Bitcoin on the Bitcoin blockchain.

Buying Bitcoin

1. Sign up for a Coin base account. Signing up for a coin base account will provide you with a secure place to keep your Bitcoin. You will also have access to an easier payment method as it allows you to convert your fiat currency into Bitcoin.

2. Link your bank account. Once you have signed up for coin base, then you will need to link it to your bank account. There will be a few verification steps that you have to go through to use your account. But, once you have completed these steps, you will be able to start buying Bitcoin.

3. Once you have completed your first purchase, you will need to ensure that you are getting your Bitcoin delivered to the proper address. Keep in mind that the price of Bitcoin will change over time.

4. Now that you have gotten the hang of buying Bitcoin, you can buy as much Bitcoin as you want. Just ensure that you are not spending too much money or else you will find that you have placed yourself between a rock and a hard place. It is wise to set a limit and do not spend more than that.

Selling Bitcoin

Selling Bitcoin will be a standard way to trade your Bitcoin. There are a few ways that you will be able to sell your Bitcoin online.

1. Direct trades: There are websites that will offer you a selling structure such as Coin base or Local Bitcoins in the United States. These sites will require you to register as a seller. The registration process will involve verifying your identity. After you have registered, you will have the option of posting offers online to show that you want to sell your Bitcoin. The website will then alert you whenever someone decides to make a trade with you. Once you accept the trade, you will be interacting with that person alone, but you will have to use the website to complete the trade.

   A United Kingdom site involves an extensive process when it comes to trading which means that you will need to be patient. Any Bitcoin users who link their accounts to their bank accounts will use Coin base or Circle since the trading process is simplified.

2. Exchange trades: You always have the option of registering when involved in an online exchange. You will still need to verify your identity, but by completing this process; you will not have to do as much work when you decide to organize a sale. Online exchanges will act as an intermediary in holding a user's funds.

To start the process of selling Bitcoins, you will place a sell order and insert the amount that you want to sell and how much you want for it. The most prominent downside will be when you sell Bitcoins for fiat currencies since the funds will have to be withdrawn from your bank. If the exchange is facing liquidity problems, then it could take an undetermined amount of time to get your money.

On the other hand, you can use a pure cryptocurrency exchange to trade Bitcoin with another cryptocurrency. It is not often that people want to go through with this option.

To top it off, you will have to pay a fee to use a few of the online exchanges. Another thing that you need to consider is how much money you will be allowed to store in the exchange. It is not recommended that you put all of your Bitcoin into the exchange because exchanges can be hacked.

Remember, you need to take control of your own funds!

Chapter Nine: Wallets

When it comes to using a wallet, the most secure wallet that you will be able to use is a hardware wallet, but they will cost money, and that is not always an option for someone who does not have a lot of money. So, if you do not have the money to get a hardware wallet, you can always choose to use a software wallet.

Let's look at some wallets so that you can see what they have to offer.

Ledger Nano S:

Similar to the Trezor wallet, Ledger is a cold wallet created to allow users to access a wallet that has a lot of security. This wallet will be a physical device you connect to your computer. You are not going to be able to send Bitcoins from your wallet unless you own the physical device, but in case you are looking for a cold wallet, this is a good one to start with.

Ledger offers a wide range of products such as Ledger Nano S, Ledger Unplugged and many others, but the most popular one is Ledger Nano S.

The best thing about Ledger is that it is user-friendly and offers excellent security.

The con that accompanies Ledger Nano S is that it is expensive because it is more secure but other than that it has no other function which is also an issue for cold wallets.

Trezor:

Trezor will be the wallet you want if you are looking store a large number of Bitcoins while keeping them out of harm's way. The world-class security and flexibility make this wallet good for everyone. Trezor company has gained a lot of traction and helpful reviews throughout the past year.

The pros of using Trezor aside from the security it offers include, supporting you in using additional wallets, allowing you to collect altcoins, and it is easy to use.

The downside of using Trezor is that it is expensive.

Coin base

Coin base is one of the leading exchange services you can find today when it comes to buying or selling Bitcoin. Coin base was founded in 2012 and has received $31 million from venture capital funding. The Bitcoin exchange service can be used in nineteen countries around the world. The online wallet that they offer is excellent for beginners but allowing your coins to stay with Coin base is risky. However, Coin base came up with a solution by launching their vault service which protects your funds from companies.

Coin base allows you to add funds from inside your wallet. Moreover, Coin base is a well-established and respectable company, and it is user-friendly.

The most prominent disadvantage is that the company will have control over your funds, and it is not supported around the world.

Blockchain.info

This Bitcoin wallet allows you to send and receive Bitcoin by using a web browser or your mobile phone which is why it is being referred to as the hybrid wallet. Hybrid wallets will store your cryptocurrency, but they don't have access to your private key. This wallet is highly recommended if you are just trying Bitcoin out to see if you want to use it.

Blockchain.info's pros are that it is a company that is trusted in the Bitcoin community, you can use it on the internet and on your phone. Moreover, the interface is easy to manipulate.

The cons are that you have to trust a third party and you are not going to have the option of making anonymous payments.

Chapter Ten: Pros and Cons of Blockchain

Blockchain has good points and bad points. You need to know the pros and cons of the system so that you can make an informed decision on what you will use blockchain for. The more knowledgeable you are regarding blockchain, the easier it is for you to manipulate it. Then, nothing will stop you from investing and taking advantage of blockchain.

Pros

1. Dissemination: One of the core values of blockchain is that it enables a database to share information without the need for a central authority. Instead of having centralized application logic, the transactions for blockchain will have their own authorization and validity acting as a consensus mechanism, so that the nodes can remain in sync and transactions can be verified while also being processed independently.

But, how will this be useful for the users of blockchain? Since the database will be a tangible thing, it is still going to be measured in bits and bytes. So, the contents of the database will be stored on the memory and the disk of the computer that is being used, even if a third party is using them. Since the data is on a computer, it can be corrupted.

Thus, a third-party organization will need to control their database by hiring people that they trust to prevent the database from being tampered with. This process will take a lot of time and money, and there is no way around it if you want to ensure that your database is secure.

With blockchain, you will be able to replace the third-party organization with a distributed database protected by cryptography.

2. Empowered: Users will be in control of the information they place on the blockchain and their transactions. This means that users have the control over their finances, and do not have to rely on someone else.

3. High data quality: Once blockchain has all of the data that it needs; then data will be consistent, timely, accurate, and always available.

4. Progress integrity: Users will be able to trust that their transactions will be executed as the protocol states; all the while ensuring a third party is not needed.
5. Transparency and immutability: Any changes that are made on the blockchain will be available for the public to see. And, all transactions are immutable so no need to worry about the transaction being altered or deleted from the chain.

Cons

1. Performance: Since the database is decentralized, the blockchain's nature includes being slower than a database that is centralized. While transactions are being processed, the blockchain has to do each operation that a regular database does with additional steps involved.

    a. Signature verification: All transactions have to be signed digitally through a public-private cryptography scheme called ECDSA. This has to occur so that transactions are propagated between nodes in a peer-to-peer fashion, or else the sources are not going to be proven. Signature generation and verification for these signatures will be computationally complicated since it will consist of a bottleneck product. However, compared to centralized databases, once the connection has been established, each request will no longer need to be verified individually.

   b. Redundancy: This is not going to refer to the performance of a single node, but the total amount of computer power that the blockchain will require to keep running. Centralized databases will process transactions only once because each node has to be prepared individually. Thus, a lot of work has to be done to achieve the same result.

2. Nascent technology: Some issues will be hard to solve such as transaction speed and data limits.

3. Uncertain regulation status: A government entity regulates most modern currencies, but blockchain and bitcoin are facing an issue regarding this because the government is uncertain as to how they would control the digital currency. This makes it extremely difficult for blockchain users.

4. Massive energy consumption: It is estimated that a blockchain miner will consume four hundred and fifty thousand trillion solutions per second to validate transactions.

5. Control, privacy, security: Solutions are available in order to resolve issues like control, privacy, and security issues that comes with blockchain, but the problem comes when working with a private blockchain that requires a lot of encryption. Plus, there are cybersecurity concerns that have to be addressed before the public allows their personal data to be used as a blockchain solution.

6. Cost: It is true that blockchain will offer a lot of savings when it comes to transaction costs, but there is a high initial capital cost that will be deterrent to some. This capital cost is due to websites that remain up and running without charging their users.

Now that you know the pros and cons of the blockchain, you will be more informed in making your investment decision. The blockchain is not going to update, but it will evolve. If you are looking for something that will upgrade, then you need to look at blockchain applications, like Ethereum.

Chapter Eleven: Blockchain and the Financial Industry

"There are hundreds of startups with a lot of brains and money working on various alternatives to traditional banking" – Jamie Dimon, JPMorgan Chase

The rules for the game of creating and capturing economic value were once set in stone, so it was easy for a company to follow the same business model while executing their business plan better than their competition. However, due to the technology, business models have been disrupted which in turn changed the nature of economic returns and industry definitions. Each and every industry is seeing a rapid displacement and sometimes even complete destruction. The financial sector has been no exception despite the fact that they have money managers.

"Silicon Valley is coming", Jamie Dimon said in his annual letter that is sent out to the shareholders. He went on to talk about startups coming for Wall Street which creates efficiency in areas that are vital to companies, like JPMorgan, especially when it comes to the business of lending money.

Payment startups, such as Strip obtained a multibillion-dollar valuation and partnerships with big companies like Apple. But, bitcoin companies and exchanges, like Coin base are pulling in millions of dollars from the venture capitalists that used to work for the traditional financial enterprises. Thanks to the peer-to-peer lending, there has been a boom in small loans. And, this has caused a lot of companies to spring forward to help keep up with the demand. One such player, known as Learn Vest was acquired for more than two hundred and fifty million dollars.

Most of these organizations will be in the business of lending money, but to keep up with the changing times they are using big data and cloud technologies for them to offer faster transactions for their customers. There are other organizations that are using network business models like peer-to-peer lending so that they can bring both lenders and borrowers together.

Dimon said, "We will work hard to make our services as seamless and competitive as theirs." It is his belief that if his company cannot keep up with these startups that are using blockchain, he will lose relevance in a world that is becoming platform-centric.

There have been a lot of innovative network business models who utilized traditional financial services but have not been able to get the help they needed. Thus, this made the big banks to realize that they need to evolve to remain a viable option for the companies that are using blockchain. Keeping up with the changes may require partnering with some of the leading-edge technologies or by creating their own. While this is a clear option for the financial service, what is not clear is why the new financial solutions are so disruptive to the traditional options that have been around for centuries. The answer is simple, the network allows for business models to be placed on a platform that will help make sure that they are doing what is best for their customers.

A team of technologists in London has attempted to understand how blockchain technologies should be used to change the future of banking worldwide. Blythe Master, an ex-Wall Street trader, has been focusing on improving business models for the financial services, along with each party that is related to the financial industry.

There have been bank executives throughout the world that have been attempting to figure out where their firms will be with the modern technology and what will happen to them should this technology takes over. "We could go the way that file transfer technology changed music, allowing new businesses like iTunes to emerge. That is why there is such feverish activity at the moment," Mr. Harte (Chief operations and Technology officer at Barclays) told the Financial Times.

Even though the financial services sector is massive, blockchain has swooped in and offered opportunities to overhaul the commercial world's existing business model, and that includes the infrastructure of banks and how they interact with their customers. Banks that act on this opportunity have been able to make the most of blockchain but the task had not been easy for them because of the core beliefs that have been reinforced in their industry, since the beginning.

As you already know, blockchain is a distributed database that will keep track of transaction records. So, instead of acting like a bank and working with a centralized authority, blocks will be approved by users; and the security will make it to where these transactions cannot be tampered with.

"It is only a matter of time before the broader financial services and banking industries shift to blockchain and network-based approaches."

So, as you have seen, blockchain is turning the financial industry upside down, and big banks have no choice but to jump on board and use blockchain or else they will end up becoming extinct. Many financial institutions are creating teams that will be able to help startups that want to use blockchain so that they can keep up with the changes occurring with technology. They are doing this because they do not want to lose their customers, but they are not ready to completely let blockchain take over.

Chapter Twelve: Blockchain Hard Forks

When you are thinking of a hard fork and how it relates to the blockchain, a radical change will occur to the protocol that causes any blocks that were previously invalid to become valid as long as all the nodes and users have upgraded to the newest protocol. Another way to think of it is that hard forks will be a permanent divergence from a previous version of blockchain. And when a node is not run by the new version, it will not be accepted anymore. This typically creates a fork in the blockchain where one path goes through the new upgrades to the blockchain, and the other continues to work with the outdated version of the blockchain. After a short period of time, the users that are still working on the old chain will realize that they are using an outdated version of blockchain and will need an upgrade.

Hard forks can be implemented to fix a security risk that has been discovered in on an older version of blockchain. Fixing might involve adding a new functionality or reversing a transaction. A hard fork will include two paths for blockchain by considering a transaction as invalid upon validation and confirmation by a node

When the DAO was hacked causing DAO to lose millions of dollars to an anonymous hacker, Ethereum's community voted for a hard fork so that transactions could be reversed. This hard fork allowed the DAO token holders to get their funds back. But, the hard fork did not unwind all of the transactions that happened on the network. Instead, it relocated the funds that were linked to the DAO since a new smart contract was created with the purpose of allowing the original owners to withdraw the money. Any DAO token holder was able to pull out ether at a rate of one ether per hundred DAO. This extra balance, along with any ether that was left resulted in a guaranteed protection for DAO.

Example of a hard fork

In the summer of 2017, news.bitcoin.com published an article about how to prepare for a fork which the bitcoin network experienced in the August 1st blockchain split. At present, there are two bitcoin forks scheduled. In the event that a division occurs when these forks occur, then there will be four blockchains that will share the same transaction history from the original blockchain.

Bitcoin Gold's project wanted to fork the network to create an Application Specific Integrated Circuit creating a resistant version of bitcoin. The reason behind forking this system was because the Bitcoin Gold team believed that the ASIC mining had become too centralized. Therefore, the developers wanted to make bitcoin mineable with a graphics processing unit, and this could be accomplished by changing the original protocol's consensus so that it would run off an algorithm called Equihash. The hard fork was scheduled to occur on October 25th, but sadly it would not be live until November 1st.

The hard fork known as Segwit2x was a technical compromise that came from the New York Agreement that happened between a majority of the miners and businesses that are on the blockchain. There are people who think that the agreement was put into place, so miners could be pushed into using their hash rate voting power in implementing the Segregated Witness protocol. However, the activation of Segwit came with an agreement that would require a two-megabyte hard fork to take place three months later. This hard fork was set to be put into place November 18th, but it would ultimately depend on the hash rate.

What happens before, during, and after a fork

There are a few things that you have to know about what happens around the time that a fork will take place. Before a fork takes place, users will need to ensure that they have put their funds in the appropriate place at the right time. So, you will either need to put your funds on the exchange or place the money in a non-custodial wallet. Many people think that the best practice is for you to remain in full control of your funds which means you need to possess your own private key.

Before the fork happens, if you decide to move your funds to a non-custodial wallet, make sure that you have set your seed phrases and that your private key is available. As long as you have the private key, you will be in control of your funds before and after the fork.

During the fork, most users will agree that making a transaction is not the best idea. You need to remain patient until the fork is over so that you can make sure that you are keeping your coins rather than forfeiting them because you got impatient. While the fork is happening, confusion is common while the blockchain reorganizes and gets back to where it is functioning correctly.

Even after the fork, you need to remain patient. Be observant and take your time, and you should investigate the infrastructure of both forks, now that the split has occurred. You should look at how to import your private keys, and how you will be able to claim split tokens as you wait for the appropriate tools to be placed where they are supposed to be.

For example, there are some bitcoin wallets that require their users to wait for app maintainers to create the proper tools or to be able to adapt to the new network. Many people wait a few days, and some even wait weeks before their wallet providers can support the split fully.

Chapter Thirteen: Blockchain and Other Industries

The financial sector is not the only industry that is being changed by blockchain. As you have seen in the earlier chapter, there is a wide range of industries that are using or are planning on using blockchain to improve their customer interactions and to make sure that they are staying seen by the public.

Let's look at a few other industries that will be changed because they decided to use blockchain.

1. Global logistics and shipping: This industry is perfect in utilizing blockchain. However, there are several layers that will be involved in the process. The product drivers, haulers, shippers, forwarders, virtually everyone that is included in the logistics and shipping of packages around the world. In fact, all of the interactions that you just read about can be downsized, therefore making the shipping procedure more efficient thanks to blockchain.

If blockchain will be utilized for logistics and shipping, then it would be more transparent and have more accountability for helping it to thrive. Blockchain has the option of allowing the public to verify products, as well as monitor the shipping process from beginning to end. A regulator is also going to be more informed and involved in the process. Plus, when a smart contract is used, there will be a better system for validation for the items that are successfully delivered.

2. Advertising: The CEO and Co-founder of Proxio was reported saying "I do not like the idea that marketing and advertising are dominated by a few players such as Facebook and Google. Perhaps we need something different since these internet giants are taking an enormous cut from the $550 billion advertising industry, while businesses receive no guarantee that their ads will convert to sales or even that their ad traffic is genuine."

However, when you look at companies like Bitclave, they want to disrupt this cycle, and they plan on using blockchain so that they can connect their customers directly to their business. Their customers will have the option of accessing the businesses' data and get paid each time their business is used. Plus, the companies will be able to personalize their offers for their customers.

3. Healthcare: When you think of healthcare, you think of your medical records, and you want those to be kept safe. By using blockchain, medical records can be kept secure, and if they need to be transferred, there is no need for the records to be printed or emailed. Instead, the new doctor will enter a password on the blockchain to access the files.
4. Real estate: The real estate sector has been plagued because of their lack of transparency, mistakes, and fraud. Even the verification process presents challenges that need to be addressed because even when all conditions are met; there still a delay in the transferring of funds.

But, by using a decentralized process alongside smart contracts, it will get rid of the need to pay an attorney while lowering closing costs. There are already platforms that are working to make the real estate industry better.

5. Forecasting: If you look at how blockchain can be used from a consulting and analysis point of view, you will see that it contains a lot of potentials in disrupting the forecasting sector. By using this technology, people will be allowed to follow and

predict elections, sports, and stocks in a decentralized environment.

Bob Marshall, the founder of WeatherBug, is under the belief that blockchain will be able to deal with meteorology and climate change, as well. Various experts that are within the forecasting industry have seen that blockchain has the potential to boost the industry in areas that deal with energy, food, and other organic resources.

6. Crowdfunding: One of the most popular methods for a startup to get money and raise awareness is through crowdfunding. However, the downside is the high fee that the platform will charge since these platforms are working as middlemen. However, what if there is no need for a middleman? What if you will be able to use smart contracts and other online reputation systems that would increase the trust that is created between investors and creators?

Thanks to crowdfunding, because now you can! By using crowdfunding, startups will have to use the blockchain to obtain the funds that they need to start their business. There has been a wide range of startups that have used crowdfunding to start their business.

One such company is known as Digix; they used blockchain and crowdfunding to get the money they needed to create Dapp. There are plenty of other industries that will be able to use blockchain to change how they run their business. But, not every industry has gotten around to realizing that they need to keep up with changing technology or else they will be destroyed. The industries that you saw listed above are using blockchain, and have noticed that it has changed their industry for the better.

Chapter Fourteen: The Impact of Blockchain

During the last year, blockchain had been under the study of the Australia Commonwealth Scientific and Industrial Research Organization by their Data61 group.

The group has a partnership with the CSIRO; they are dedicated in locating, designing, and studying data innovations. The reports that they recently published have announced that the blockchain is a "highly promising" method to manage supply chains for the financial industry, governments, and other industries as a way to increase the productivity of Australia. And thus,

which could end up causing Australia to be placed at the forefront of the technology and enterprise race. However, the CSIRO also said that blockchain will have its own vulnerabilities that users will need to be aware of if they will invest on the blockchain.

Data61 was commissioned by the Australian Treasurer, Scott Morrison, to work with input obtained from the government and industries that can be found in Australia. Being that they are already a leader in blockchain technology, Morrison advised the Australian government and businesses that they should use the reports as "guidance on how they can accelerate their take up on blockchain technology."

The Data61 group reported and illustrated the profound impact that blockchain would have when it comes to the security, productivity, and efficiency gains in the Australian economy.

These reports also showed details of case studies that were executed on blockchain applications for government registries, remittance payments, and even trade finances. But, some warnings could be found in the studies about how the encryption needed to be broken by a fast enough computer. However, the hyped technology was going to be put at risk of being corrupted, compromising the blockchain privacy, creating other security concerns, or breaching blockchain confidentiality.

The reports that can be found from Data61's study were intended to advise businesses in how blockchain technology would help them in identifying their risks and discovering if it would be worth it for them to use it. At the same time, the reports were presenting scenarios that the government would be able to look at when the possible pitfalls of using a digital economy occurred if they fail to move fast enough and adapt to the evolving technology.

A primary principle that Data61 advised its blockchain regulators involved
the importance of technological neutrality when it came to using blockchain, as well as providing indicative guidance for the evaluation of blockchain proposals.
There is a major concern that comes from mixing technology and businesses because there are some that believe privacy will be put at risk. Since the data that is on the blockchain cannot be tampered with, there is no such thing as "toxic data" or data that is considered maliciously entered. Therefore, there won't be any legal issues when it comes to a contract being examined or the data being removed from the chain.

Yet another concern for blockchain users will be that the application is not future proof. For example, the speed that you see in quantum computing can break through the encryption that is currently placed on the blockchain, thus making it vulnerable.

On top of that, Data61 pointed out that blockchain is not the best when it comes to dealing with large-scale databases. Because of this, big data has to be placed in the chain while a fully utilized blockchain is operated by another IT system. Moreover, a person has to ensure that all of the computing needs for the blockchain are being met.

The last thing that you should consider is how blockchain can be used for some organizations since how they plan to use the system will make it more expensive for them. Data61 discovered that the blockchain system would be tested under the best possible conditions, but it may not take into account the possibility of complicated situations.

The CEO of Data61 said that "regardless of its limitations, blockchain is here to stay and Australia is well placed to be the first to benefit from the technology. Blockchain can drive operational efficiency and structural change for the country. Specifically, in food provenance and personalized healthcare applications."

When being used for supply chains, blockchain was not just integrating the information, but it was improving the operational efficiencies throughout the industry, as well as improving the quality of the supply chain. Blockchain was able to facilitate the source of goods that were branded, as well as reduce the costs linked to regulatory approvals according to a Data61 report.

Craig Laundy (Assistant Minister of Industry, Innovation, and Science) stated that "the blockchain technology could reduce costs for businesses, especially where it concerns shipping and payments. One of the greatest cost-saving and security avenues are the rates of fraud in food importation between China and Australia. This ultimately has the potential for our producers here to ensure the integrity of their supply chains internationally through foreign trade."

Despite the fact that blockchain has a bad reputation because of bitcoin and the dark web, the future of blockchain and the business of Australia is at a crossroad. Companies are to the point where they either have to choose to invest and thrive, or ignore the blockchain and ultimately perish. If Australia gets to lead the way in making blockchain standard, then they will be able to help other countries around the world, since they will be living proof of how blockchain works.

A partner at King and Wood Mallesons by the name of Scott Farrell who helped Data61 said, "Blockchain's capabilities to ensure trust between business partners must be understood by those companies if they want to strengthen their standings."

Mr. Staples, also with Data61, wrote in a report, "Australia would end up relying on blockchain-based systems for lots of reasons given the huge economic value in the form of efficiencies. But, it is much too early to quantify what those will be. Critically, for those considering the technology from either a tactical or strategic perspective, the reports provide a scientific foundation for making decisions, not only on what the technology is and what it can do, but where it might lead us and how we might get there."

Another consultant for Data61 reported, "the technology is primarily about productivity and if endorsed by various governments would bolster GDP growth, which typically increases people's trust."

When you examine Australia's economy, you will see that there is an unknown number of businesses that are considering using blockchain applications. There have been several banks that are willing to get on board with blockchain, as well. There is even a startup by the name of AgriDigital that created a ledger to assist in eliminating the risk that occurs by a grain buyer against the grain growers.

The chief executive of Australian Digital Currency and Commerce Association stated, "Australian regulators have been fast in responding to the onset of digital currency, mentioning the recent lifting of double goods and services tax on digital currencies."

Nicholas Giurietto also imported that the government in Australia was going to create a task force that would only work at overseeing the adoption of blockchain so that there are no accidental legal barriers that have to be dealt with and that each business to invest with blockchain can retain technological neutrality.

"Australia now has a clear picture of how blockchain technology could transform our economy in the coming decades. We now need to make a choice to accelerate our efforts, or see other countries overtake us while we pay the price for moving too slowly," Giurietto said.

Conclusion

Thank you for making it through to the end of *Blockchain: Everything You Need to Know About Blockchain*. Let's hope it was informative and was able to provide you with all of the tools you need to achieve your goals whatever it may be.

The next step is to find the blockchain application that you want to use. With the blockchain application, you will be using a value token such as bitcoin or ether. Also, choose the best wallet that can provide you with high security and smooth, user-friendly interface.

You may find some issues when using blockchain, but take note that, there is nothing that you will be able to do about them except to let the developers know so that they can add it to their list of what needs to be fixed.

Let's face it, Bitcoin is still new. As it continues to develop, we should expect technical problems. That means using Bitcoin will not always be sunshine and rainbows, but we can be confident that as the time passes by, Bitcoin will come close to perfection. We can expect major improvements in this digital currency in the future. Again, the best way to deal with the issues that you may face is to report it to the developers.

When you report a problem, you need to be patient because blockchain developers are always fixing issues so that they can provide a better platform for users to have access to. Not only that, but they are humans too, and they are not going to be working twenty-four seven. Be patient, and believe that your problem will be fixed!

If you are unable to reach the developers, seek help from Bitcoin professionals. You can do so by either contacting a cryptocurrency expert or by joining discussions in different forums. Other people might be able to help you with the problem you're having.

The actual blockchain is not going to change except through hard forks. But, the applications for blockchain will evolve so that the users will have everything that they want out of the platform so that they would not look for other platforms to use.

The first step in using these applications is to understand the concept of blockchain, and hopefully, in this book, you were able to learn enough about blockchain that you won't have too many problems when you begin using it.

No doubt, understanding cryptocurrency, how Bitcoin works, and how this platform revolves, can be very difficult. It's complicated and hard to understand at first. So, to fully learn and benefit from cryptocurrency, read as much information as you can. Before investing, make sure you know what you are into.

Finally, if you found this book useful in any way, a review on Amazon is always appreciated!

Thank you and good luck!

Description

In the past few years, blockchain has become more popular. Thanks to bitcoin and Ethereum. To begin using these applications, you have to know how to use blockchain, and what better time to start than now?

The future of blockchain is unknown, but it appears that blockchain technologies are beginning to take over some major industries utilized by the general public. And being able to use this technology will place you a step above those that do not understand the technology.

Thousands of people around the world are now using Bitcoin. Many have doubted the capabilities of this digital currency, but Bitcoin has proved that it can be the future of the finance world.

You should not delay learning about blockchain. Even if you do not use it right away, knowing how to use it will benefit you sooner or later.

In this book you will learn:

1. What the blockchain is and how it works.

2. The future of blockchain.

3. The pros and cons of blockchain, so that you can make informed investing decisions.

4. How blockchain is changing the financial industry.

5. The impact of blockchain.

And so much more!

So, why are you still putting off learning blockchain? Pick up this book now, and begin changing your future!

www.ingramcontent.com/pod-product-compliance
Lightning Source LLC
Chambersburg PA
CBHW071422220526
45469CB00004B/1385